Guide to Winning Email Marketing

Practical Guide

G. Dellis

Copyright © 2024

Guide to Winning Email Marketing

1.Introduction to Email Marketing

Email marketing is one of the most effective and direct digital marketing strategies for communicating with your target audience. Since the advent of the Internet, email has been a powerful medium for sending commercial, promotional, and informational messages to a selected group of recipients. When executed correctly, this approach can lead to a significant increase in sales, customer loyalty, and brand recognition. In this guide, we will explore the various aspects of email marketing, from its definition to its benefits, best practices, and how to implement a successful campaign.

1. What is Email Marketing?

Email marketing involves sending commercial messages using email. These messages can include a variety of content such as promotional offers, company updates, newsletters, event invitations, surveys, and more. The main goal is to build and maintain relationships with customers, increase brand awareness, and drive sales and conversions.

1.1 Types of Email Marketing

There are different types of emails that a company can send:

- **Newsletters**: Sent regularly, they contain news, updates, and interesting articles for the recipients.

- **Promotional Emails**: Offer discounts, special offers, or information about new products.

- **Transactional Emails**: Sent in response to a customer's action, such as order confirmations or shipping notifications.

- **Engagement Emails**: Aim to keep customers interested through personalized and relevant content.

- **Re-engagement Emails**: Designed to

reactivate inactive users by offering incentives or requesting feedback.

2. Advantages of Email Marketing

Email marketing offers numerous advantages over other marketing methods:

- **Cost-Efficiency**: It is relatively inexpensive compared to traditional marketing campaigns such as TV or print advertising.

- **Wide Reach**: Allows you to reach a large audience quickly and directly.

- **Personalization**: Messages can be highly personalized based on user data, increasing the effectiveness of campaigns.

- **Measurability**: Email marketing platforms offer detailed analytics tools to monitor campaign performance.

- **Immediacy**: Emails can be sent and received almost instantly, allowing for timely communication.

3. Creating an Email Marketing Strategy

To successfully implement an email marketing campaign, it is essential to follow a well-defined strategy. Here are the main steps:

3.1 Defining Objectives

Before starting, it is important to establish the goals of the campaign. Common goals include:

- Increasing sales
- Generating leads
- Improving customer retention
- Driving traffic to the website
- Promoting new products or services

3.2 Building the Contact List

A qualified contact list is crucial for the success of email marketing. Here are some ways to build it:

- **Sign-up Forms**: Strategically placed on the website or social media.

- **Lead Magnets**: Offering valuable content (eBooks, webinars, etc.) in exchange for a subscription.

- **Events and Trade Shows**: Collect contacts during live events.

3.3 Audience Segmentation

Segmentation allows you to divide the contact list into homogeneous groups based on specific criteria such as:

- Demographics (age, gender, location)

- Behavior (purchase history, previous email interactions)

- Interests (stated preferences)

This approach enables more targeted and relevant messages, increasing the chances of success.

3.4 Creating Content

The content of the emails must be attractive and relevant to the recipients. Here are some tips:

- **Compelling Subject Line**: The subject line is the first element the recipient sees; it must capture attention and entice them to open the email.

- **Responsive Design**: The email should be easily readable on all devices, including smartphones and tablets.

- **Call to Action (CTA)**: Every email should have a clear and visible CTA that guides the user towards the desired action.

3.5 Automation and Personalization

Automation allows emails to be sent efficiently and timely. Some examples of automated emails include:

- **Welcome Emails**: Automatically sent when a new user subscribes to the list.

- **Abandoned Cart Reminders**: Sent to those who have added products to the cart without completing the purchase.

- **Post-Purchase Follow-ups**: To thank customers and request feedback.

Personalization can greatly enhance engagement. Using the recipient's name, sending recommendations based on previous purchases, or offering exclusive discounts can make a significant difference.

4. Tools and Platforms for Email Marketing

There are numerous platforms that offer advanced tools for managing email marketing. Some of the most popular include:

- **Mailchimp**: One of the best-known platforms, offering automation, segmentation, and analytics features.

- **Constant Contact**: Known for its support and ease of use, ideal for small businesses.

- **Sendinblue**: Offers comprehensive email marketing and automation solutions at competitive prices.

- **HubSpot**: An all-in-one platform that integrates email marketing with CRM and other digital marketing tools.

These platforms provide pre-defined templates, drag-and-drop editors, and integrations with other marketing and CRM tools, making it easier to create and manage campaigns.

5. Measuring the Success of Email Marketing

To understand if an email marketing campaign is effective, it is essential to monitor and analyze a series of key metrics:

- **Open Rate**: Percentage of emails opened compared to those sent.

- **Click-Through Rate (CTR)**: Percentage of recipients who click on one or more links in the email.

- **Conversion Rate**: Percentage of recipients who complete the desired action (purchase, subscription, etc.).

- **Bounce Rate**: Percentage of emails not delivered.

- **Unsubscribe Rate**: Percentage of recipients who unsubscribe from the list.

Analyzing these metrics allows you to understand what works and what doesn't, and to make adjustments to improve future campaigns.

6. Best Practices for Email Marketing

To maximize the effectiveness of email marketing campaigns, it is important to follow some best practices:

- **Compliance**: Ensure that you have explicit consent from recipients and provide an easy way to unsubscribe.
- **Optimal Frequency**: Avoid sending emails too frequently to prevent annoying recipients.
- **A/B Testing**: Experiment with different versions of emails to understand what works

best.

- **Clarity and Conciseness**: Messages should be clear and direct, focusing on the value for the recipient.

- **Continuous Monitoring and Optimization**: Analyze performance and make ongoing adjustments.

7. Examples of Successful Campaigns

Observing successful campaigns can offer inspiration and useful insights. Here are some examples:

- **Netflix**: Uses personalized emails to suggest content based on users' tastes and viewing habits.

- **Amazon**: Sends product recommendation emails based on previous purchases and shown interest.

- **Airbnb**: Uses emails with personalized content to promote destinations and experiences, increasing user engagement.

8. Challenges of Email Marketing

Despite the numerous advantages, email marketing also presents challenges:

- **Spam**: Avoiding emails ending up in the spam folder is crucial for success.

- **Competition for Attention**: In an age of information overload, capturing the recipient's attention can be difficult.

- **Managing Unsubscribes**: Keeping a clean list and managing unsubscribes is essential for maintaining a good sender reputation.

Email marketing remains one of the most powerful and versatile tools in the digital marketing landscape. With a well-defined strategy, the use of appropriate tools, and attention to best practices, businesses can fully exploit the potential of emails to achieve their business goals. Continuously monitoring results and adapting campaigns based on received feedback is key to maintaining high effectiveness and staying competitive in an ever-evolving market.

2. Importance of Email Marketing for Businesses

Email marketing has evolved as a fundamental

component in the marketing strategies of modern businesses. This tool offers a direct and personal way to communicate with the target audience, and if well implemented, it can bring significant benefits in terms of customer loyalty, increased sales, and enhanced brand visibility. In this detailed discussion, we will explore the importance of email marketing for businesses, analyzing various aspects such as return on investment (ROI), personalization, automation, integration with other marketing strategies, and best practices to maximize campaign effectiveness.

1. Return on Investment (ROI)

One of the main reasons why businesses continue to invest in email marketing is its high return on investment (ROI). Studies have shown that email marketing can generate a significantly higher ROI compared to other forms of digital marketing. According to the Direct Marketing Association, every dollar spent on email marketing can yield an average return of $42. This makes email marketing one of the most cost-effective tools.

1.1 Cost Efficiency

Email marketing requires a relatively low initial investment compared to other forms of advertising, such as television or social media campaigns. Email marketing platforms offer a range of packages that can fit various budgets, making this tool accessible even to small businesses.

1.2 Measurability and Analysis

Email marketing platforms provide detailed analytics tools that allow businesses to monitor and measure the performance of their campaigns in real time. Metrics such as open rate, click-through rate (CTR), conversion rate, and unsubscribe rate help evaluate the effectiveness of sent emails and make adjustments to improve future performance.

2. Personalization and Segmentation

Personalization is one of the most powerful aspects of email marketing. Personalized emails tend to have higher open and click rates than generic ones. Modern email marketing platforms allow businesses to collect and analyze customer data, enabling them to create tailored messages for each audience segment.

2.1 Audience Segmentation

Segmenting the contact list means dividing it into homogeneous groups based on specific criteria such as demographics, purchasing behaviors, interests, and previous interactions. This approach allows for sending more relevant and targeted messages, increasing the likelihood of engagement and conversion.

2.2 Dynamic Content

The use of dynamic content in emails allows for further personalization of messages based on specific recipient data. For example, an email can include product recommendations based on a customer's previous purchases or contain personalized special offers. This level of personalization can significantly improve the customer experience and strengthen the brand relationship.

3. Marketing Automation

Automation is another key element of email marketing that enhances its effectiveness. Marketing automation platforms allow for scheduling and sending emails in response to certain actions or events, improving the timeliness and relevance of communications.

3.1 Welcome Emails

Welcome emails are automatically sent when

a new user subscribes to the list. These emails are crucial for making a good first impression and can include useful information on how to use products or services, welcome offers, and invitations to follow the brand on social media.

3.2 Abandoned Cart Reminders

Abandoned cart reminder emails are designed to recover lost sales. These emails are automatically sent to those who have added products to their cart but have not completed the purchase, offering incentives such as discounts or free shipping to encourage checkout completion.

3.3 Post-Purchase Follow-Up

Follow-up emails sent after a purchase can improve customer loyalty and increase repeat sales. These emails can include feedback requests, tips on using purchased products, or special offers for future purchases.

4. Integration with Other Marketing Strategies

Email marketing does not work in isolation; it can be integrated with other marketing strategies to amplify overall results.

4.1 Synergy with Social Media

Email marketing campaigns can be enhanced with social media. For example, emails can include invitations to follow the company on social media or share user-generated content. Additionally, social media can be used to collect email addresses through promotions or contests.

4.2 Support for Content Marketing Campaigns

Email marketing can support content marketing campaigns by distributing valuable content directly to recipients' inboxes. Newsletters, for example, can include blog articles, videos, eBooks, and other useful content that educates and engages the audience.

4.3 Events and Webinars

Emails can be used to promote events and webinars, increasing participation and engagement. Personalized invitations and automated reminders can help maintain interest and ensure good attendance.

5. Customer Loyalty

Another significant advantage of email marketing is its ability to improve customer loyalty. Regular and personalized communications can keep customers engaged and interested in the brand.

5.1 Loyalty Programs

Emails can be used to manage and promote loyalty programs. Informing customers about their accumulated points, exclusive offers, and special benefits can incentivize loyalty and increase repeat sales.

5.2 Regular Newsletters

Regular newsletters keep customers informed about company news, special offers, and valuable content. This type of communication helps keep the brand in the customers' minds and build a long-term relationship.

5.3 Customer Feedback

Emails can be used to collect feedback from

customers, thereby improving the products and services offered. Asking for customers' opinions shows that the company values their feedback and can lead to significant business improvements.

6. Best Practices for Email Marketing

To get the most out of email marketing, it is important to follow some best practices that can improve campaign effectiveness and ensure compliance with regulations.

6.1 Compliance with Regulations

Regulations such as GDPR (General Data Protection Regulation) require businesses to obtain explicit consent from recipients before sending marketing emails. It is essential to ensure that data collection and list management practices comply with these regulations to avoid penalties and protect the company's reputation.

6.2 Relevant Content

The content of emails must be relevant and valuable to the recipients. Generic or irrelevant messages can lead to unsubscribes and reduce the overall effectiveness of campaigns. Segmentation and personalization are crucial for creating content that resonates with the audience.

6.3 Clear Calls to Action

Each email should have a clear and visible call to action (CTA). Whether it is to purchase a product, sign up for a webinar, or download an eBook, the CTA must be easily identifiable and understandable to recipients.

6.4 Testing and Optimization

A/B testing is a common practice in email marketing to understand which version of an email works best. Testing different subject lines, layouts, CTAs, and content can provide valuable insights into what resonates most with the audience and improve the performance of future campaigns.

6.5 Monitoring and Analysis

Monitoring campaign metrics and analyzing collected data is essential to understand the effectiveness of email marketing strategies. The information gathered can be used to make adjustments and optimize future campaigns, ensuring continuous improvement.

3. Define the Objectives of Your Email Marketing Campaign

Defining objectives is the first and most crucial step in planning a successful email marketing campaign. Clear and well-defined objectives not only provide direction for your campaign but also help measure and evaluate the results achieved. In this guide, we will explore how to identify and define email marketing campaign objectives, the different types of objectives you can consider, and strategies to achieve them effectively.

1. Importance of Defining Clear Objectives

Before diving into the details, it is important to understand why defining clear objectives is fundamental:

- **Direction and Focus**: Objectives provide clear direction and help focus resources and efforts on what is truly important.

- **Measurability**: Without clear objectives, it becomes difficult to measure the campaign's success and understand what works and what doesn't.

- **Team Motivation**: Well-defined objectives can motivate the team, providing a clear vision of what is to be achieved.

- **Optimization**: Knowing the objectives allows you to optimize ongoing and future campaigns to continuously improve results.

2. Types of Objectives for an Email Marketing Campaign

Email marketing campaign objectives can vary greatly depending on the specific needs of the company and the target audience. Here are some of the most common types of objectives:

2.1 Increase Sales

One of the most common objectives of email marketing campaigns is to increase sales. This can be done through special offers, seasonal promotions, new product launches, and more.

- **Promotions and Discounts**: Send emails with special offers and discounts to encourage purchases.

- **New Product Launches**: Inform customers about new products and encourage them to make a purchase.

- **Cross-Selling and Upselling**: Suggest complementary or higher-value products based on previous customer purchases.

2.2 Lead Generation

Email marketing campaigns can be used to generate new leads, i.e., potential customers interested in your products or services.

- **Webinar or Event Registration**: Invite recipients to participate in webinars, events, or seminars to collect contact information.

- **Content Download**: Offer eBooks, white papers, or guides in exchange for signing up to your email list.

- **Surveys and Quizzes**: Use surveys or quizzes to engage recipients and gather contact information.

2.3 Customer Retention

Retaining existing customers is often more cost-effective than acquiring new ones. Email marketing can help improve customer retention.

- **Loyalty Programs**: Promote loyalty programs and rewards to encourage repeat purchases.

- **Follow-Up Emails**: Send follow-up emails after a purchase to request feedback and suggest related products.

- **Regular Newsletters**: Keep customers informed about news, offers, and valuable content through regular newsletters.

2.4 Increase Website Traffic

Driving traffic to the website is a common objective for many email marketing campaigns.

- **Blog Articles and Content**: Share blog articles, videos, and other content to encourage recipients to visit the site.

- **Exclusive Promotions**: Offer exclusive promotions that require visiting the website to redeem.

- **Online Event Invitations**: Invite recipients to participate in online events, such as webinars or live streaming.

2.5 Increase Brand Awareness

Email marketing campaigns can be used to improve brand awareness and build a stronger presence in the market.

- **Customer Stories**: Share testimonials and success stories from customers.

- **Branding Initiatives**: Send emails that tell the brand's story, company values, and social responsibility initiatives.

- **Collaborations and Sponsorships**: Inform recipients about collaborations with other companies or event sponsorships.

2.6 Improve Customer Engagement

Improving customer engagement is crucial for maintaining a solid and lasting relationship.

- **Interactive Content**: Use interactive content like surveys, quizzes, and games.

- **Personalization**: Send personalized

emails based on customer behaviors and preferences.

- **Feedback Requests**: Ask recipients to leave reviews or feedback on products or services.

3. How to Define SMART Objectives for Email Marketing Campaigns

An effective methodology for defining clear and achievable objectives is the use of SMART goals. SMART is an acronym that stands for Specific, Measurable, Achievable, Relevant, and Time-bound.

3.1 Specific

Objectives must be clear and specific. A vague goal like "increase sales" is not sufficient. Instead, a specific goal might be "increase sales by 20% through promotional email campaigns in the next quarter."

3.2 Measurable

Objectives must be measurable to assess progress. For example, "increase the email open rate by 10% within six months" is a measurable goal.

3.3 Achievable

Objectives must be realistic and achievable. Setting overly ambitious goals can lead to frustration and demotivation. It's important to consider the resources available and the company's capabilities.

3.4 Relevant

Objectives must be relevant to your company and aligned with your overall business goals. For example, if your main goal is to increase sales, focusing efforts on acquiring new customers might be more relevant than increasing website traffic.

3.5 Time-bound

Objectives must have a clear deadline. For example, "increase the number of newsletter subscribers by 15% by the end of the year" is a time-bound goal.

4. Examples of SMART Objectives for Email Marketing

Here are some examples of SMART objectives you might consider for your email marketing campaigns:

- **Increase Sales**: "Increase sales by 25% through a promotional email campaign within the next three months."

- **Lead Generation**: "Increase the number of webinar sign-ups by 30% through invitation emails within six weeks."

- **Customer Retention**: "Reduce the unsubscribe rate by 10% through personalized monthly newsletters within a year."

- **Increase Website Traffic**: "Increase blog traffic by 20% by sending weekly emails with interesting articles within six months."

- **Increase Brand Awareness**: "Increase brand mentions on social media by 15% through emails promoting content sharing within three months."

- **Improve Customer Engagement**: "Increase the click-through rate on emails by 10% by implementing interactive and personalized content within the next quarter."

5. Strategies to Achieve Objectives

Defining objectives is only the first step. It is equally important to develop strategies and action plans to achieve them. Here are some effective strategies:

5.1 Contact List Segmentation

Segmentation allows you to send targeted messages to specific groups of recipients, increasing the relevance and effectiveness of emails. For example, you can segment your list based on demographic data, purchase behaviors, interests, or customer lifecycle stages.

5.2 Content Personalization

Personalized emails, which include the recipient's name or recommendations based on previous purchases, tend to have higher open and click rates. Use the information at your disposal to create content that resonates with your recipients.

5.3 A/B Testing

A/B testing involves creating two versions of an email and sending them to small segments of your list to see which version performs better. This allows you to optimize the subject line, design, content, and CTAs of your emails to maximize results.

5.4 Email Automation

Automation allows you to send relevant and timely emails based on user actions. For example, you can set up welcome emails for new subscribers, reminders for abandoned carts, or post-purchase follow-ups.

5.5 Creating Valuable Content

Emails must offer value to recipients to maintain high engagement. This can include educational content, exclusive offers, product updates, or anything else that your customers find useful and interesting.

5.6 Mobile Optimization

With more people reading emails on mobile devices, it is essential to ensure that your emails are optimized for viewing on smartphones and tablets. Use responsive design and test them on various devices to ensure an optimal user experience.

6. Monitoring and Analyzing Results

Monitoring and analyzing the results of your campaigns is crucial to understanding whether you are achieving your objectives and making necessary adjustments.

6.1 Key Metrics

Here are some key metrics you should monitor:

- **Open Rate**: The percentage of recipients who open your emails. A high open rate indicates that your subject lines are effective and that your audience is interested in your messages.

- **Click-Through Rate (CTR)**: The percentage of recipients who click on links within your emails. This measures the effectiveness of the content and CTAs.

- **Conversion Rate**: The percentage of recipients who perform the desired action (e.g., make a purchase, sign up for a webinar). This is one of the most important metrics for evaluating your campaign's success.

- **Unsubscribe Rate**: The percentage of recipients who unsubscribe from your list. A high unsubscribe rate can indicate that your emails are not relevant or that you send too many emails.

- **Bounce Rate**: The percentage of emails that cannot be delivered. A high bounce rate can indicate problems with the quality of your contact list.

6.2 Analysis Tools

There are various tools and platforms that can help you monitor and analyze your email marketing campaigns, such as Google Analytics, Mailchimp, HubSpot, and others. Use these tools to gather detailed data and gain useful insights.

6.3 Reporting and Optimization

Create regular reports to evaluate your campaign performance and identify areas for improvement. Use this data to optimize future campaigns, test new strategies, and continuously improve results.

7. Adaptation and Continuous Improvement

Marketing is a dynamic field, and what works today may not work tomorrow. It is essential to remain flexible and ready to adapt to changes.

7.1 Customer Feedback

Listen to your customers and gather feedback on your emails. This can provide valuable insights into what works and what needs improvement.

7.2 Market Trends

Stay updated on the latest marketing trends and new technologies. Adapting your strategies based on new trends can give you a competitive advantage.

7.3 Innovation

Don't be afraid to experiment with new ideas and approaches.

Innovation can lead to new opportunities and improved results.

Conclusion

Defining clear and measurable objectives is the foundation of a successful email marketing campaign. By understanding the various types of objectives, setting SMART goals, and implementing effective strategies, you can maximize the impact of your email marketing efforts and achieve your desired results. Remember to continuously monitor, analyze, and optimize your campaigns to stay ahead of the competition and adapt to changing market conditions.

4. Creating a High-Quality Contact List for Email Marketing

Creating a high-quality contact list is one of the most important components for the success of an email marketing campaign. A well-curated contact list can lead to higher open rates, more conversions, and better customer retention. This process requires a well-defined strategy and the implementation of various tactics to ensure that the collected contacts are genuinely interested in the products or services offered. In this article, we will explore in detail how to create a high-quality contact list for email marketing, considering best practices and the most effective strategies.

1. Importance of a High-Quality Contact List

Before examining the techniques for creating a high-quality contact list, it is essential to understand why it is so important to have a high-quality list.

- **Higher Open and Click Rates**: Qualified contacts are more likely to open your emails and interact with the content.

- **Lower Unsubscribe Rate**: A well-curated list reduces the risk of recipients unsubscribing, keeping your subscriber base high.

- **Better Sender Reputation**: Emails sent to qualified contacts are less likely to be marked as spam, improving your reputation with email service providers (ESPs).

- **Better ROI**: The resources invested in email marketing generate a better return on investment when emails reach interested and engaged recipients.

2. Strategies for Creating a High-Quality Contact List

2.1 Offering Valuable Content

One of the most effective ways to attract qualified subscribers is by offering valuable content. This can include:

- **Ebooks and Guides**: Create ebooks or in-depth guides on topics relevant to your target audience and offer them in exchange for signing up to your email list.

- **Webinars and Online Events**: Organize webinars on topics of interest to your audience and require email sign-up to participate.

- **White Papers and Reports**: Publish detailed white papers and reports that offer valuable information to your audience and require sign-up to access them.

2.2 Using Effective Sign-Up Forms

The sign-up form is a crucial tool for collecting qualified contacts. Here are some best practices for optimizing sign-up forms:

- **Strategic Placement**: Place the sign-up form in visible areas of the website, such as the header, footer, or as a pop-up.

- **Clarity and Simplicity**: Ensure that the form is clear and easy to fill out. Only request essential information to reduce friction.

- **Clear Call to Action (CTA)**: Use CTAs that clearly explain the value of signing up, such as "Subscribe for exclusive updates."

2.3 Offering Incentives

Incentives can be a powerful motivator to encourage users to sign up for your email list. Here are some examples:

- **Discounts and Exclusive Offers**: Offer an immediate discount or an exclusive offer for new subscribers.

- **Contests and Giveaways**: Organize contests and giveaways where signing up to the email list is a requirement to participate.

- **Early Access**: Provide early access to new products or exclusive content for newsletter subscribers.

2.4 Leveraging Social Media

Social media is a powerful platform to promote your email contact list and reach a wider audience.

- **Paid Promotions**: Use sponsored ads on social media to promote your sign-up incentives.

- **Shareable Content**: Create content that encourages sharing and includes a sign-up invitation.

- **Integrations**: Use integration tools to add sign-up forms directly on social media pages.

2.5 Optimizing the Website

Your website is one of the most important resources for collecting contacts. Here's how to optimize it:

- **Dedicated Landing Page**: Create dedicated landing pages for collecting sign-ups, focusing on a single call to action.

- **Exit-Intent Pop-Up**: Use pop-ups that appear when the user is about to leave the site, offering an incentive to sign up for the email list.

- **Blog Content**: Include invitations to sign up for the newsletter within blog articles, offering added value content.

3. Management and Maintenance of the Contact List

Once contacts are collected, it is essential to manage and maintain the list to ensure its quality.

3.1 Email Verification

Use email verification tools to ensure that the collected addresses are valid and active. This reduces the risk of high bounce rates and improves the sender's reputation.

3.2 List Segmentation

Segment the contact list based on specific criteria such as demographics, purchase behavior, interests, and customer lifecycle stage. Segmentation allows for sending more relevant and personalized emails, improving engagement and conversions.

3.3 List Cleaning

Periodically remove inactive or unengaged

contacts. Keeping a clean list improves deliverability and reduces the costs associated with sending emails to inactive contacts.

3.4 A/B Testing

Conduct A/B tests on different aspects of emails (subject lines, content, layout) to understand what works best and continuously optimize your campaigns.

4. Best Practices for Contact Collection

To ensure that collected contacts are of high quality, follow these best practices:

4.1 Informed Consent

Ensure that contacts provide explicit consent to receive emails from you. This is not only a best practice but also a legal requirement in many jurisdictions (e.g., GDPR in Europe).

4.2 Transparency

Be transparent about what subscribers can expect to receive. Clearly explain the email frequency and the type of content that will be sent.

4.3 Unsubscribe Option

Always provide a clear and easy option to unsubscribe from emails. This helps maintain a genuinely interested and engaged contact list.

5. Success Stories

Examining case studies of companies that have successfully created high-quality contact lists can offer valuable insights and inspiration. Here are some examples:

5.1 HubSpot

Strategy: HubSpot uses a combination of valuable content (eBooks, guides, webinars) and well-placed sign-up forms to collect qualified contacts.

Result: Thanks to a strong content marketing strategy and the use of effective sign-up forms, HubSpot has built a highly qualified contact list and significantly increased its conversion rate.

5.2 Dropbox

Strategy: Dropbox offered free storage space as an incentive for signing up to the newsletter and for sharing with friends.

Result: This approach led to rapid growth of the contact list and helped Dropbox expand its user base exponentially.

5.3 Neil Patel

Strategy: Neil Patel uses high-quality content (blog, eBooks, webinars) and well-positioned pop-ups to collect sign-ups. Additionally, he segments the contact list to send highly personalized emails.

Result: The combination of valuable content and segmentation has allowed Neil Patel to maintain a high open and engagement rate in his email campaigns.

6. Tools and Resources for Contact Collection

Using the right tools can simplify the process of collecting and managing contacts. Here are some useful tools:

6.1 Email Marketing Platforms

- **Mailchimp**: Offers advanced features for creating sign-up forms, list segmentation, and email automation.

- **Constant Contact**: Great for small businesses, with easy-to-use tools for collecting contacts and sending emails.

- **HubSpot**: A comprehensive platform that includes tools for contact collection, email campaign management, and detailed analytics.

6.2 Email Verification Tools

- **NeverBounce**: Verifies the validity of email addresses to reduce bounce rates.

- **ZeroBounce**: Another effective tool for verifying and cleaning contact lists.

6.3 Sign-Up Form Plugins

- **OptinMonster**: A powerful tool for creating pop-ups, slide-ins, and other customizable sign-up forms.

- **Sumo**: Provides a variety of options for sign-up forms and contact collection tools.

7. Monitoring and Analyzing Results

After implementing your strategies, it is crucial to monitor and analyze the results to understand what works and what doesn't.

7.1 Metrics to Monitor

- **List Growth Rate**: Monitor how quickly your contact list is growing.

- **Open and Click Rates**: Measure email

engagement.

- **Conversion Rate**: Evaluate how many contacts perform the desired action after receiving the emails.

- **Unsubscribe Rate**: Check how many people unsubscribe after receiving the emails.

7.2 Analysis Tools

- **Google Analytics**: Can be integrated with your email marketing platform to track contact behavior after clicking on emails.

- **Email Marketing Platform Dashboard**: Most email marketing platforms offer detailed dashboards to monitor campaign performance.

7.3 Feedback and Improvements

Collecting feedback from contacts can provide valuable insights on how to improve your email marketing campaigns. Use surveys, ask for opinions on content, and evaluate responses to continuously optimize your strategies.

Creating a high-quality contact list for email marketing requires time, effort, and a well-defined strategy. By offering valuable content, using effective sign-up forms, offering incentives, and leveraging social media, you can build a qualified and engaged contact list. Managing and maintaining the list is essential to keep it clean and relevant, while monitoring and analyzing results will help you continuously optimize your campaigns. By following these best practices, you can create a high-quality contact list that will significantly contribute to the success of your email marketing strategies.

5. Creating an Effective Email and Software to Use in Email Marketing

Email marketing
is one of the most powerful tools in digital marketing, capable of reaching a wide audience at a relatively low cost. However, to make the most of this channel, it is essential to create effective emails that capture recipients' attention and encourage them to take action. This article provides a detailed guide on how to create an effective email and which software to use to optimize your email marketing campaigns.

1. Importance of an Effective Email

An effective email can:

- **Increase Open Rates**: Through captivating subject lines and preheaders.

- **Enhance Engagement**: With relevant and personalized content.

- **Generate Conversions**: Thanks to well-placed and clear call-to-actions (CTAs).

- **Strengthen Customer Relationships**: By providing added value and maintaining constant communication.

2. Key Elements of an Effective Email

Creating an effective email requires attention to various elements that make up the email itself.

2.1 Email Subject Line

The subject line is the first thing the recipient sees and can determine whether the email will be opened.

- **Be Clear and Concise**: The subject line should be short but descriptive.
- **Create Urgency**: Use words that suggest

immediate action, such as "limited offer".

- **Personalization**: Including the recipient's name or relevant information can increase the open rate.

2.2 Preheader

The preheader is the text that appears right after the subject line in inboxes.

- **Support the Subject Line**: It should complement and reinforce the message of the subject line.

- **Be Brief**: Keep it short but informative.

2.3 Design and Layout

Good design and layout can significantly improve the effectiveness of an email.

- **Responsive Design**: Ensure the email is optimized for all devices, especially mobile.

- **Use of Images**: Images should be high-quality and relevant but should not slow down the email loading time.

- **Visual Hierarchy**: Use headers, subheaders, and bullet points to make the email easy to read.

- **Color and Typography**: Colors should align with the branding, and typography should be readable.

2.4 Content

Content is the heart of your email. It must be relevant and valuable to the recipient.

- **Personalization**: Use recipient data to personalize the content.

- **Clarity and Relevance**: Content should be clear, direct, and relevant to the target audience.

- **Storytelling**: Telling a story can engage the reader more effectively.

2.5 Call-to-Action (CTA)

The CTA is the element that prompts the recipient to take a specific action.

- **Be Direct**: The CTA should be clear and indicate exactly what the recipient should do.

- **Strategic Placement**: It should be highly visible and strategically placed within the email.

- **Engaging Text**: Use action verbs that prompt action, such as "Learn More" or "Buy Now".

2.6 Footer

The footer is the final section of the email,

often overlooked but very important.

- **Contact Information**: Always include your company's contact information.

- **Social Media Links**: Provide the option to connect through social media.

- **Unsubscribe Option**: Include a clear link to unsubscribe, as required by law.

3. Best Practices for Creating Emails

3.1 Audience Segmentation

Segmenting the audience allows for sending more relevant emails.

- **Demographics**: Segment by age, gender, geographical location.

- **Behavior**: Segment based on past behaviors, such as previous purchases or email interactions.

- **Interests**: Segment based on specific interests indicated by recipients.

3.2 Personalization

Personalization can significantly improve open and engagement rates.

- **Names**: Include the recipient's name in the subject and body of the email.
- **Dynamic Content**: Use dynamic content that changes based on recipient data.
- **Personalized Recommendations**: Offer products or content based on past interests and behaviors.

3.3 Automation

Automation allows sending relevant and

timely emails without manual intervention.

- **Welcome Emails**: Send a series of welcome emails to new subscribers.

- **Abandoned Cart Reminders**: Remind customers to complete their purchase.

- **Post-Purchase Follow-Up**: Send thank you emails and request feedback after a purchase.

3.4 A/B Testing

A/B testing is essential for optimizing emails.

- **Subject Lines**: Test different versions of subject lines to see which gets a higher open rate.

- **Content**: Test different variations of content to see which engages recipients more.

- **CTAs**: Test different CTAs to see which gets the most clicks.

3.5 Legal Compliance

Ensure emails comply with laws and regulations, such as the GDPR in Europe.

- **Consent**: Obtain explicit consent from recipients to send emails.
- **Privacy Policy**: Include a link to the privacy policy.
- **Unsubscribe Option**: Always provide a clear option to unsubscribe.

4. Software for Email Marketing

4.1 Mailchimp

Description: Mailchimp is one of the most popular email marketing platforms, known for its ease of use and powerful automation features.

- **Key Features**: Advanced segmentation, automation, A/B testing, detailed analytics.

- **Pricing**: Offers a free plan with limited features and paid plans starting at $9.99 per month.

4.2 HubSpot

Description: HubSpot is an all-in-one marketing platform that includes a powerful email marketing tool.

- **Key Features**: Integrated CRM, advanced automation, personalization, detailed analytics.

- **Pricing**: Offers a free plan with basic features and paid plans starting at $50 per month.

4.3 Constant Contact

Description: Constant Contact is another widely used email marketing platform, especially popular with small businesses.

- **Key Features**: Drag-and-drop email editor, automation, social media integration, reporting.
- **Pricing**: Plans starting at $20 per month.

4.4 SendinBlue

Description: SendinBlue is an email marketing platform that also offers SMS marketing capabilities.

- **Key Features**: Advanced automation, segmentation, A/B testing, SMS marketing.
- **Pricing**: Free plan with limited sends and paid plans starting at $25 per month.

4.5 ActiveCampaign

Description: ActiveCampaign is known for its powerful automation features and integrated CRM.

- **Key Features**: Advanced automation, integrated CRM, segmentation, personalization.
- **Pricing**: Plans starting at $15 per month.

4.6 GetResponse

Description: GetResponse offers a wide range of marketing tools in addition to email marketing, including webinars and landing pages.

- **Key Features**: Email marketing, automation, webinars, landing pages.

- **Pricing**: Plans starting at $15 per month.

4.7 Klaviyo

Description: Klaviyo is particularly appreciated by e-commerce businesses for its powerful automation and personalization features.

- **Key Features**: Advanced automation, personalization, detailed analytics, integration with e-commerce platforms.
- **Pricing**: Plans starting at $20 per month.

6. Personalizing Your Emails in Email Marketing

Email personalization is a crucial element for the success of email marketing campaigns. In a digitally overloaded world, personalized emails can help stand out, increase open and click rates, and enhance overall engagement with your audience. This article will delve into how to personalize your emails, best practices to follow, and the software that can facilitate this process.

1. Importance of Email Personalization

Personalizing emails goes beyond merely including the recipient's name in the subject or body of the message. A well-executed personalization strategy can:

- **Increase Open Rates**: Personalized emails have a higher open rate compared to generic ones.

- **Improve Click Rates**: Relevant and tailored content tends to receive more clicks.

- **Boost Conversions**: Emails that address the specific needs of the recipient are more likely to generate conversions.

- **Enhance Customer Loyalty**: A personalized experience strengthens customer relationships and increases brand loyalty.

2. Email Personalization Techniques

2.1 Utilizing Recipient Data

Collecting and using recipient data is fundamental to effectively personalize emails.

- **Demographic Data**: Information such as name, age, gender, and geographic location can be used to segment the audience and tailor messages.

- **Purchase Behavior**: Analyzing past

purchase behavior can help send personalized recommendations.

- **Interests and Preferences**: Gathering data on recipients' interests and preferences through surveys or subscriptions can help create more relevant content.

2.2 Contact List Segmentation

Segmenting your contact list is one of the most important steps for sending personalized emails.

- **Demographic Segmentation**: Divide the list based on demographic criteria like age, gender, and location.

- **Behavioral Segmentation**: Create segments based on recipient behavior, such as past purchases, email interactions, or website visits.

- **Customer Journey Stage Segmentation**: Send different emails depending on the stage of the customer journey, such as new subscribers, regular customers, or former customers.

2.3 Content Personalization

Personalizing email content can be done in various ways using the collected information about recipients.

- **Names and Personal Information**: Include the recipient's name and other personal information in the emails.

- **Product Recommendations**: Use purchase behavior data to suggest relevant products.

- **Dynamic Content**: Create content blocks that change depending on the recipient, such as personalized offers or messages based on specific interests.

- **Triggered Emails**: Send automatic emails in response to specific recipient behaviors, such as cart abandonment or product purchases.

2.4 Personalizing the Subject Line and Preheader

The subject line and preheader are the first things recipients see. Personalizing them can significantly increase open rates.

- **Recipient's Name**: Include the recipient's name in the subject line.

- **References to Past Behaviors**: Refer to past purchases or recent interactions of the recipient.

- **Exclusive Offers**: Promise exclusive content or offers in the preheader.

3. Best Practices for Email Personalization

3.1 Data Collection and Management

To effectively personalize emails, it's essential to collect and manage recipient data accurately and securely.

- **Detailed Signup Forms**: Use signup forms that collect useful information such as name, age, interests, and preferences.
- **Surveys and Polls**: Conduct surveys and polls to gather additional information about recipients.
- **Analytics Tools**: Use analytics tools to monitor recipient behavior and gather relevant data.

3.2 Effective Segmentation

Segmentation should be continuous and based on updated data.

- **Regular Updates**: Regularly update segments based on new data collected.

- **Testing and Optimization**: Conduct A/B tests on different segments to understand which works best.

- **Segment Refinement**: Refine segments over time by combining various criteria to create increasingly specific groups.

3.3 Advanced Personalization

Use advanced personalization techniques to further enhance email effectiveness.

- **Automation**: Implement automated workflows that send personalized emails in response to specific recipient behaviors.

- **Dynamic Content**: Use dynamic content that changes based on recipient data.

- **Artificial Intelligence**: Implement AI solutions to analyze recipient data and automatically generate personalized content.

4. Email Personalization Software

There are numerous software options available to help you personalize your emails effectively. Below are some of the most popular and powerful email marketing tools.

4.1 Mailchimp

Description: Mailchimp is a widely used email marketing platform known for its ease of use and powerful personalization features.

- **Personalization Features**: Advanced segmentation, automation, dynamic content, product recommendations.

- **Integrations**: Integrates with numerous e-commerce and CRM platforms.

- **Pricing**: Free plan available, paid plans starting at $9.99 per month.

4.2 HubSpot

Description: HubSpot is an all-in-one marketing platform that includes a powerful email marketing tool.

- **Personalization Features**: Integrated CRM, advanced segmentation, automation, content personalization.

- **Integrations**: Wide range of integrations with other marketing and sales tools.

- **Pricing**: Free plan available, paid plans starting at $50 per month.

4.3 ActiveCampaign

Description: ActiveCampaign is known for its powerful automation capabilities and integrated CRM.

- **Personalization Features**: Advanced

automation, integrated CRM, dynamic segmentation, personalized content.

- **Integrations**: Integrates with numerous e-commerce platforms and marketing tools.

- **Pricing**: Plans starting at $15 per month.

4.4 Klaviyo

Description: Klaviyo is particularly favored by e-commerce businesses for its powerful personalization and automation features.

- **Personalization Features**: Advanced automation, behavioral segmentation, product recommendations.

- **Integrations**: Strong integration with e-commerce platforms like Shopify, WooCommerce, and BigCommerce.

- **Pricing**: Free plan available, paid plans starting at $20 per month.

4.5 GetResponse

Description: GetResponse offers a wide range of marketing tools in addition to email marketing, including webinars and landing pages.

- **Personalization Features**: Automation, segmentation, dynamic content, advanced personalization.
- **Integrations**: Wide range of integrations with e-commerce and CRM tools.
- **Pricing**: Plans starting at $15 per month.

4.6 SendinBlue

Description: SendinBlue is an email marketing platform that also offers SMS marketing features.

- **Personalization Features**: Automation, segmentation, dynamic content, behavior-based personalization.

- **Integrations**: Numerous integrations with e-commerce and CRM tools.

- **Pricing**: Free plan available, paid plans starting at $25 per month.

5. Examples of Personalized Emails

5.1 Personalized Welcome Emails

Description: Welcome emails are the first contact with new subscribers and can be personalized to make a good impression.

- **Personalization Elements**: Recipient's name, product suggestions based on interests, links to relevant content.

- **Example**: "Hi [Name], welcome to our community! Here are some resources you might be interested in: [Links to content]. Also, we've selected these products for you: [Product suggestions]."

5.2 Abandoned Cart Reminders

Description: Abandoned cart reminder emails can recover potential sales.

- **Personalization Elements**: Recipient's name, products in the cart, special offers or discounts.

- **Example**: "Hi [Name], we noticed you left some items in your cart. Here's a special offer just for you: [Discount]. Complete your purchase now: [Link to cart]."

5.3 Product Recommendations

Description: Emails with product recommendations can increase sales by showing relevant items to customers.

- **Personalization Elements**: Recipient's name, recommendations based on past purchases, exclusive offers.

- **Example**: "Hi [Name], based on your previous purchases, we think you might be interested in these products: [Recommendations]. Take advantage of this exclusive offer: [Discount]."

5.4 Birthday Emails

Description: Birthday emails are a way to show appreciation to customers and offer them something special.

- **Personalization Elements**: Recipient's name, birthday wishes, special offers or discounts.

- **Example**: "Happy birthday, [Name]! To celebrate, we're offering you a 20% discount on our entire store. Use the code: [Discount Code]."

6. Monitoring and Analyzing Personalized Emails

To evaluate the effectiveness of personalized emails, it is essential to monitor and analyze performance.

6.1 Key Metrics

- **Open Rate**: Percentage of emails opened.

- **Click Rate**: Percentage of recipients who click on links in the email.

- **Conversion Rate**: Percentage of recipients who complete the desired action (purchase, subscription, etc.).

- **Unsubscribe Rate**: Percentage of recipients who unsubscribe from the list.

6.2 Analysis Tools

- **Google Analytics**: Can be integrated with email marketing platforms to track recipient behavior after clicking on emails.

- **Email Marketing Platform Dashboard**: Most email marketing platforms offer detailed dashboards to monitor campaign performance.

6.3 Recipient Feedback

Collecting feedback from recipients can provide valuable insights on how to improve personalized emails.

- **Post-Campaign Surveys**: Ask recipients what they liked and what could be improved.

- **Response Analysis**: Evaluate responses to personalized emails to understand what works best.

Email personalization is a key component for the success of email marketing campaigns. By using advanced personalization, segmentation, and automation techniques, you can create emails that resonate with recipients, increase engagement, and improve conversions. With the help of powerful email marketing tools and the implementation of best practices, you can continuously optimize your email marketing strategies to achieve the best possible results.

7. Utilize catchy subject lines in Email Marketing

In the world of Email Marketing, subject lines are crucial for capturing the recipient's attention and motivating them to open the message. A catchy subject line should be short, clear, intriguing, and above all, convincing. Here are some tips and best practices for creating effective subject lines:

1. Be clear and specific: The subject line should clearly and directly communicate the email's content. Avoid generic or ambiguous phrases and opt for simple, understandable language.

Example 1: "Special offer just for you: -30% off all products!"

2. Use keywords: Keywords are essential for grabbing the recipient's attention. Use words that evoke interest and curiosity, such as

"exclusive," "unmissable," "discounted," etc.

Example 2: "Discover the exclusive offer reserved for our top customers!"

3. Be creative and original: Dull and repetitive subject lines risk going unnoticed. Be creative with puns, alliterations, or surprising phrases.

Example 3: "Crazy discounts: go crazy with our offers too!"

4. Use urgency and deadlines: If the email contains a limited-time offer, use the deadline to prompt the recipient to open the message immediately.

Example 4: "Last hour: 50% discount only for today!"

5. Personalize the subject line: Using the

recipient's name or personal information can increase engagement and the likelihood of email opening.

Example 5: "Hi Luca, we have a surprise for you!"

6. Test and optimize subject lines: Before sending the email, test different versions of the subject line to determine which generates the highest open rate. Use analytics tools to monitor performance and make any necessary adjustments.

Example 6: "Discover our exclusive promotion" vs "Don't miss out: -20% only for a few hours!"

Finally, remember that an effective subject line is one that sparks curiosity, interest, and urgency to open the email. Experiment, test, and optimize to find the winning formula that maximizes the open and conversion rates of your Email Marketing campaigns.

8. Testing and optimizing your emails

Email marketing is a powerful tool for reaching your customers and potential clients, but only if your emails are well-written, well-designed, and well-optimized. Testing and optimizing your emails is crucial to maximize their impact and ensure they achieve their goals.

Here are some tips for testing and optimizing your emails:

1. Subject line and preview text: The subject line and preview text are the first things recipients see when they receive your email, so they need to be captivating and engaging. Ensure you use persuasive language and create a sense of urgency or curiosity to encourage people to open your email.

2. Structure and design: Make sure your email is well-structured and easy to read. Use short

paragraphs, bullet points, and bold text to emphasize important information. Also, ensure your email design aligns with your brand and is optimized for mobile viewing.

3. Content: The content of your email should be relevant, interesting, and useful to your recipients. Include a clear call-to-action that tells recipients what to do after reading your email, such as visiting your website, making a purchase, or contacting you for more information.

4. A/B testing: A/B testing is a very useful technique for testing different versions of your email to discover which performs better. You can test different subject lines, designs, content, and calls-to-action to understand what works best for your audience and optimize your future email marketing campaigns.

5. Segmentation: Audience segmentation is crucial for sending targeted and personalized emails. Use your customer data to divide your

audience into smaller groups and send them specific content that is most relevant to them. This will increase engagement and conversion rates.

6. Monitoring and analysis: Monitor email metrics such as open rate, click-through rate, and conversion rate closely. Use this information to analyze the performance of your emails and make any necessary improvements. Also, be sure to test different variables to understand what resonates best with your audience.

Practical Example:

Imagine you have an online clothing store and want to send an email marketing campaign to promote your new spring/summer collection. Here's how you could test and optimize your emails:

1. Subject line and preview text: Test different

versions of the subject line and preview text to see which generates the highest open rate. For example, you could test "Discover the new spring/summer collection" versus "20% discount on the new collection."

2. Structure and design: Ensure your email is well-structured and visually appealing. Use high-quality images of your collection and make sure the call-to-action stands out to prompt recipients to take action.

3. Content: The content of your email should focus on your new collection, with details about fashion trends, materials used, and prices. Be sure to include a clear call-to-action directing recipients on how to purchase the products.

4. A/B testing: Test two versions of your email, one with a 10% discount and one with a 20% discount, to see which generates the higher conversion rate. Use this data to optimize future email marketing campaigns.

5. Segmentation: Segment your audience based on purchasing preferences, so you can send personalized emails to those interested in specific products or styles. For example, send shoe-related emails to customers who have purchased footwear in the past.

6. Monitoring and analysis: Monitor email metrics and analyze the data to determine which performs best. Use this information to make improvements to your future email marketing campaigns.

Testing and optimizing your emails is essential to maximize their impact and improve the performance of your email marketing campaigns. Follow the tips outlined above and use the practical examples to create effective and engaging emails that generate positive results for your business.

9. Analyzing the results of your email marketing campaign

After launching my email marketing campaign, it's time to analyze the results to understand how effective it was and what actions we can take to improve future performance.

The first step is to analyze basic metrics such as open rates, clicks, and conversions. These data will give us a general idea of how engaging our campaign was for recipients and whether it generated concrete results.

The open rate is a fundamental metric that tells us how many people actually opened our email. A high open rate is a positive sign that our subject line and email content are appealing to the audience. If the open rate is low, it may indicate that we need to work on these aspects to make our emails more compelling.

Click-through rate is another important metric that tells us how many people clicked on links within the email. A high click-through rate indicates that our message sparked interest and motivated recipients to interact with our website or landing page. If the click-through rate is low, we can test different types of calls-to-action or modify the email layout for better results.

However, the most important metric is conversion rate. This data tells us how many recipients actually took the action we wanted them to take, such as making a purchase or signing up for a service. If the conversion rate is low, we may need to review our sales funnel or checkout process to simplify the customer experience and increase conversions.

In addition to basic metrics, it's also important to analyze other data such as bounce rate and recipient segmentation. Bounce rate indicates how many emails were not successfully delivered and could be due to technical issues or an outdated email list. Keeping our contact list clean is crucial for optimal email delivery.

Recipient segmentation is another crucial aspect to consider. Segmenting our audience into groups based on interests, behaviors, or demographics allows us to send more targeted and personalized messages, thereby increasing engagement and conversion rates. We can use email marketing automation tools to create customized communication flows for each audience segment.

After analyzing the data from our email marketing campaign, we can draw conclusions and suggestions for improving future performance. For example, we could test different email subject lines to understand which ones generate more opens, or enhance the design and formatting of the email to make the content more visually appealing.

Additionally, we could experiment with different types of content such as videos, customer testimonials, or special offers to see which ones generate more interest and interaction. By constantly monitoring metrics and conducting A/B tests, we can continuously optimize our email marketing campaigns to maximize results.

Finally, it's important to consider recipient feedback and monitor engagement on social media to assess the impact of our campaign. Make sure to respond to recipient comments and questions and seize opportunities for interaction to build deeper relationships with the audience.

Analyzing the results of our email marketing campaign is essential to understand what worked and what we can improve. By using collected data to make informed decisions and experimenting with different approaches, we can optimize our performance and achieve better results over time.

10. Lead generation

Lead generation is one of the most important components of email marketing, essential for acquiring new potential customers and growing your business. It's a fundamental process through which qualified contacts are captured—those who have shown interest in the brand or the products/services offered—with the goal of converting them into actual customers.

To effectively tackle the lead generation phase in email marketing, it's important to follow some effective tips and strategies that can maximize results and increase the chances of success. Firstly, it's crucial to define who your potential customers are and what their needs and interests are. This allows you to create targeted and personalized email campaigns that grab attention and generate interest.

Another crucial aspect is using compelling and clear call-to-actions. In every email sent, it's important to include a call-to-action that prompts the recipient to take action, such as clicking a link to get more information, downloading an ebook, or requesting a product demo. The call-to-action should be prominently displayed and strategically positioned within the email.

Another effective strategy for lead generation in email marketing is creating personalized and optimized landing pages. A well-designed landing page can significantly increase lead conversion by providing detailed information about the product/service offered and encouraging visitors to provide their contact information in exchange for something valuable, such as a free webinar or an exclusive discount.

Furthermore, it's important to consider the importance of database segmentation. Dividing contacts based on demographic, behavioral, or interest criteria allows for sending more personalized and targeted email campaigns, increasing the chances of generating qualified leads and acquiring new customers.

Finally, it's essential to monitor and analyze the results of email marketing campaigns to assess the effectiveness of the strategies employed and make any necessary improvements. Using analytics tools like Google Analytics or monitoring features offered by email marketing platforms allows tracking recipient behavior, understanding which content is most appreciated, and optimizing future lead generation campaigns.

To make the strategies described clearer and more concrete, below is a practical example of how you could structure a lead generation campaign in email marketing:

Email subject: Discover the new product X and receive an exclusive 20% discount!

Email body:

Good morning [Recipient's name],

We are excited to introduce you to our latest product X, designed specifically to meet your needs and enhance your experience. And if you make a purchase by the end of the month, you can benefit from an exclusive 20% discount!

Click the link below to learn more about product X and take advantage of the special offer:

[Call-to-action: Discover product X]

Also, if you would like more information or to book a free demo, please don't hesitate to contact us. We are here to assist and support you every step of the way.

Thank you for your attention and have a great day!

Best regards,

The [Company Name] Team

In conclusion, lead generation in email marketing is a fundamental process for the growth and success of your business. By following the strategies and tips described above, you can maximize the effectiveness of your email marketing campaigns and generate qualified leads ready to become loyal customers. It's important to experiment and test different strategies to understand what works best for your target audience and constantly adapt your lead generation strategies.

11. Effective Examples of Email Marketing Texts

Email marketing is one of the most effective strategies for promoting your products or services, generating qualified leads, and increasing sales. To ensure that your email marketing campaigns are truly effective, it's important to write engaging, personalized, and relevant emails for your target audience. Below are 40 effective examples of email marketing, accompanied by details and tips on how to best write them:

1. Subject: "Welcome to our community!"

   Text: Hi [Name], thank you for subscribing to our newsletter. Discover the latest news and exclusive promotions!

2. Subject: "Dear [Name], discover our new spring-summer collection!"

   Text: Hi [Name], we present to you our new spring-summer collection. Explore this season's trends and take advantage of special discounts just for you!

3. Subject: "You left something in your cart!"

   Text: Hi [Name], you forgot something in your cart. Enjoy your 10% discount to complete your purchase!

4. Subject: "Get 20% off your next purchase!"

   Text: Hi [Name], enjoy a 20% discount on your next purchase. Don't miss out on this unbeatable offer!

5. Subject: "Take our survey and discover the gift we have for you!"

   Text: Hi [Name], take our survey and discover the gift we have reserved for you. We want to better understand your needs to offer you a more personalized service!

6. Subject: "Discover 5 new recipes with our

products!"

Text: Hi [Name], we present to you 5 new recipes you can prepare with our products. Also, discover tips from our chefs!

7. Subject: "30% discount just for you!"

Text: Hi [Name], we're giving you a 30% discount on all our products. Take advantage of this unbeatable offer now!

8. Subject: "Feeling like traveling? Discover our special offers!"

Text: Hi [Name], feeling like traveling? Discover our special offers and book your next vacation now!

9. Subject: "Update your wardrobe with the latest trends!"

Text: Hi [Name], we present to you the latest seasonal trends. Update your wardrobe and discover perfect outfits for you!

10. Subject: "Download our free guide and discover the secrets to success!"

Text: Hi [Name], download our free guide and discover the secrets to success in your industry. Don't miss the opportunity to improve your performance!

11. Subject: "Join our free webinar!"

Text: Hi [Name], join our free webinar and discover the latest industry updates. Take this opportunity to gain new skills!

12. Subject: "Discover our Black Friday deals!"

Text: Hi [Name], Black Friday is approaching and we have prepared unbeatable offers for you. Don't miss the chance to make great deals!

13. Subject: "Discover the 10 tips for a healthy life!"

Text: Hi [Name], we present to you the 10 tips for a healthy and fit life. Follow our advice and improve your lifestyle!

14. Subject: "Receive a special gift for your birthday!"

Text: Hi [Name], we want to celebrate your birthday with you. Receive a special gift from us and enjoy your day!

15. Subject: "Need personalized advice?"

Text: Hi [Name], need personalized advice? Contact us and our expert will help you find the best solution for your needs!

16. Subject: "Discover our best-selling products!"

Text: Hi [Name], we present to you our best-selling products. Discover which ones are our customers' favorites and add them to your cart!

17. Subject: "Have you tried our new menu?"

Text: Hi [Name], have you tried our new menu? Discover the delicious new items we have prepared for you and book your table now!

18. Subject: "Renew your subscription and get a 20% discount!"

Text: Hi [Name], renew your subscription and get a 20% discount. Don't miss this fantastic opportunity!

19. Subject: "Discover our loyalty program and earn points for great rewards!"

Text: Hi [Name], discover our loyalty program and earn points with every purchase. Get fantastic rewards and exclusive discounts!

20. Subject: "Enter our contest and win a fantastic prize!"

Text: Hi [Name], enter our contest and you could win a fantastic prize. Follow the instructions and keep your fingers crossed!

21. Subject: "Discover the best offers of the month!"

Text: Hi [Name], we present to you the best offers of the month. Take advantage of discounts and special promotions just for you!

22. Subject: "Receive our product catalog and choose the perfect gift for you!"

Text: Hi [Name], receive our product catalog and choose the perfect gift for you. You'll find a wide selection of quality items!

23. Subject: "Discover the 10 golden rules for perfect makeup!"

Text: Hi [Name], we present to you the 10 golden rules for perfect makeup. Follow our tips and create a fabulous look!

24. Subject: "Sign up for our online course

and gain new skills!"

Text: Hi [Name], sign up for our online course and acquire new skills in your industry. Don't miss this opportunity for professional growth!

25. Subject: "Take advantage of our free delivery service!"

Text: Hi [Name], take advantage of our free delivery service. Order your favorite products now and have them delivered to your home!

26. Subject: "Need assistance? Contact us now!"

Text: Hi [Name], need assistance? Contact us now and our representative will be ready to help you resolve any inquiries!

27. Subject: "Discover our tips for a perfect trip!"

Text: Hi [Name], we present to you our tips for a perfect trip. Plan your vacation down to the smallest detail and have an unforgettable experience!

28. Subject: "Subscribe to our newsletter and receive a 15% discount on your next purchase!"

Text: Hi [Name], subscribe to our newsletter and get a 15% discount on your next purchase. Stay updated on our promotions and news!

29. Subject: "Discover the latest fashion trends for the upcoming season!"

Text: Hi [Name], we present to you the latest fashion trends for the upcoming season. Update your look and follow your style!

30. Subject: "Join our affiliate program and earn with us!"

Text: Hi [Name], join our affiliate program and start earning with us. Become our partner and maximize your business opportunities!

31. Subject: "Take advantage of the Early Bird offer for our upcoming event!"

Text: Hi [Name], take advantage of the Early Bird offer for our upcoming event. Reserve your spot now and save on the ticket cost!

32. Subject: "Discover the secrets to a balanced diet!"

Text: Hi [Name], we present to you the secrets to a balanced diet. Follow our tips and maintain your health at its best!

33. Subject: "Receive our free sample kit and discover our products!"

Text: Hi [Name], receive our free sample kit and discover our products. Take this opportunity to try the quality of our items!

34. Subject: "Have you tried our personalized shopping service?"

Text: Hi [Name], have you tried our personalized shopping service? Contact us and our personal shopper will be ready to help you find the perfect look for you!

35. Subject: "Discover the beauty secrets of the stars!"

Text: Hi [Name], we present to you the beauty secrets of the stars. Follow our tips and achieve a red carpet look!

36. Subject: "Receive 50% off your next purchase!"

Text: Hi [Name], we're giving you a 50% discount on your next purchase. Take advantage of this incredible promotion and shop without limits!

37. Subject: "Sign up for our training course and achieve new professional milestones!"

Text: Hi [Name], sign up for our training course and achieve new professional milestones. Invest in your growth and succeed in your industry!

38. Subject: "Discover the new features of our app!"

Text: Hi [Name], we present to you the new features of our app. Download it now and discover all the new updates we have prepared for you!

39. Subject: "Have you tried our online personal shopping service?"

Text: Hi [Name], have you tried our online personal shopping service? Contact us and our personal shopper will be ready to help you find the perfect look for you!

40. Subject: "Discover the 5 reasons to choose our products!"

Text: Hi [Name], we present to you the 5 reasons to choose our products. Discover the quality, originality, and reliability of our items —you won't be able to do without them!

These examples will help you create engaging and personalized emails for your target audience. Remember to constantly test your email marketing campaigns to identify the most effective strategies to achieve your marketing goals.

Index

1. Introduction to Email Marketing pg.4

2. Importance of Email Marketing for Businesses pg.17

3. Define the Objectives of Your Email Marketing Campaign pg.28

4. Creating a High-Quality Contact List for Email Marketing pg.45

5. Creating an Effective Email and Software to Use in Email Marketing pg.60

6. Personalizing Your Emails in Email Marketing pg.73

7.Utilize catchy subject lines in Email Marketing pg.90

8.Testing and optimizing your emails pg.94

9.Analyzing the results of your email marketing campaign pg.99

10.Lead generation pg.103

11.Effective Examples of Email Marketing Texts pg.108

www.ingramcontent.com/pod-product-compliance
Lightning Source LLC
Chambersburg PA
CBHW071933210526
45479CB00002B/665